THE MANAGING YOUR POCKETBOOK

By Max A. Eggert

Drawings by Phil Hailstone

This Pocketbook is dedicated to Steve Dorian at P&O Services, Michele Jackson at TAB (NSW), Rohanne Young at AMSA and Elizabeth Dunbavan at Booz Allen & Hamilton without whom my first consulting year in Australia would have been very different indeed!

"An easily read and understood guide, packed with information and tips which will help readers achieve the best results from their appraisal interview." **Katie M. M. Rae, Education and Development Manager, Royal College of Nursing Institute, Scotland**

"An excellent and handy tool. Covers the whole appraisal process and can be used either as a step-by-step guide or for referencing particular aspects. Just what busy managers need - whether they are appraising or being appraised." **Chris Bunker, Manpower, Careers & Performance Development Manager, Cathay Pacific Airways, Hong Kong**

CONTENTS

INTRODUCTION

WHOSE JOB IS IT ANYWAY?

When you think about it, who has the most to gain from doing your job? **You**, of course!

The organisation gains because employment is not an exercise in charity, but you gain more - not only financially but also regarding job satisfaction from discovering how to do the best you can.

More importantly, good job performance is the key to success and promotion. Failures and average performance do not earn promotion.

WHY APPRAISAL?

If you don't know **what** you are supposed to be doing and, more importantly for appraisal, if you don't know **how** you are doing, you could be running very hard, doing your very best but going in the wrong direction.

When putting effort into something as important as work, it is essential for you to know what is required of you and how well you are performing.

INTRODUCTION

HELP YOUR MANAGER HELP YOU

Most managers find appraisal difficult. Some don't want to play God and judge you, and poor managers don't have the interpersonal skills required to appraise properly.

Some managers use excuses such as: 'You've been doing the job for some time so you should know what's required by now'. Yes, you would if you had a crystal ball at your work station and a broomstick in the corner!

This Pocketbook shows you how to help your manager help you - in improving job performance, maximising your promotion prospects and in helping you achieve your career ambitions.

Whatever your aspirations you are not likely to achieve them without effort (unless your parents own the organisation). **Appraisal is one of the ways you can help yourself achieve what you want out of your job, your career and your working life.**

APPRAISEE BENEFITS

ALL TO YOUR ADVANTAGE

8. Improving your job

1. Objectivity

2. Information about your job

7. Agreeing your objectives

ALL TO YOUR ADVANTAGE

3. Feedback on your performance

6. Improving your training & development

5. Improving your pay & benefits

4. Establishing your career potential

6

APPRAISEE BENEFITS

1. OBJECTIVITY

Appraisal when executed properly will ensure that you and your work are measured and judged fairly. Appraisal is a far better system than one based on:

Favouritism   The person with the bluest eyes wins

Seniority   The person with the longest service always gets the promotion or the benefits

Serendipity   The person who happens to be around at the right time wins

Popularity   The person with the biggest smile wins

Attractiveness   The person with the most sex appeal wins

Good appraisal is based on how well you do your job against predetermined standards of performance and quality related to the overall objectives of your department, unit and organisation.

APPRAISEE BENEFITS

2. INFORMATION ABOUT YOUR JOB

If your work is going to be appraised you need to know as much as possible about what you are supposed to be doing so that you can do a good job. You need to know:

- What the standards of output are
- What the standards of quality are
- What resources you can use to help you
- What resources you can ask for to help you
- Where you can get support and assistance
- Where you can get further training to help you

Put simply, if you don't know what you are supposed to do it is unlikely that you will be able to do it. All of us tend to do what we want and like to do rather than what we are supposed to do. If we are not told what is expected of us we will quite naturally fall back to doing what we like best.

3. FEEDBACK ON YOUR PERFORMANCE

You cannot improve unless you know how you are doing. An essential part of appraisal is to give you feedback, measured against:

- Objective standards of output
- Objective standards of quality
- The performance of others doing the same job
- The expectations of your manager
- The values and culture of your organisation

Note
Within the context of appraisal, it is important to note that negative feedback does not mean you are doing anything wrong. Should this be the case, there is the disciplinary procedure and appraisal has nothing at all to do with this.

4. ESTABLISHING YOUR CAREER POTENTIAL

Appraisal is an opportunity to explore with your manager where you see yourself going and jobs where you feel you could make a significant contribution.

However, be prepared for performance feedback that may be at variance with your own opinions. Painful though this is, such information is essential in achieving your goals. It enables you to change your behaviour so that you can perform better. (See the section on feedback and the Johari Window, pages 61-70)

Your aspirations must be realistic. Your manager, having privileged information (eg: about competition for your intended post) can help here.

The major benefit to you of appraisal is the opportunity to declare your intentions. If you don't ask you don't get. You'll be surprised what you can get when you ask!

5. PAY & BENEFITS

Not all appraisal systems deal directly with pay, bonus and benefits but increasingly organisations are linking these to performance.

Your appraisal will help you understand your pay/bonus level and will provide a forum to discuss and review matters. Appraisal is **not**, however, the place for negotiation; there should be other procedures for dealing with pay appeals.

Appraisal should help you to understand the organisation's remuneration policy and how it applies specifically to you. You will be helped, through feedback, to do better and eventually this should have an effect on your pay and/or performance bonus - even if appraisal and remuneration are two separate systems in your organisation.

APPRAISEE BENEFITS

6. TRAINING & DEVELOPMENT

Once you have information on what is required and how you are performing, you will know what training and support you will need to become more effective and productive. Appraisal is an opportunity to ask for what you think you need but make sure you can justify the training in terms of the requirements of your job.

Obviously your manager will have views on what training may or may not be appropriate, depending on budgetary constraints and work priorities.

Remember, the most effective training is `on the job'. How you might use your job to develop your skills and experience can be discussed and agreed during your appraisal interview. Your manager is ideally placed to help. This will make your job more interesting and increase your value to the organisation.

7. AGREEING YOUR OBJECTIVES

Which would you prefer: to be told what is expected of you in the next period, or to discuss and agree your objectives before they are established?

Most people would prefer to have their thoughts and ideas taken into consideration first. Since you are doing the job you will have a very good idea about what is possible and what is not, and even more idea about how you would like to approach any objectives or requirements for the future. Objectives usually fall into three basic categories:

Performance & Quality   What needs to be achieved and to what standard

Systems & Processes   How to improve what gets done and the way it gets done

Personal Development   What you need to do to improve your skills and expand your experience

8. IMPROVING YOUR JOB

All jobs can be improved and this should be a continual process. As you know your job better than most, you are ideally placed to make suggestions for efficiency, quality and improved performance. The organisation benefits but you gain job satisfaction and interest. Also, the more healthy the organisation, the more job security for you.

Appraisal allows you to discuss your job content with your manager. Obviously, the more senior you are the easier it is to accommodate your requests and build the job around your skills and abilities. It is really helpful for your manager to know which aspects of your job you find particularly attractive.

MANAGEMENT BENEFITS

GETTING THE BEST FROM PEOPLE

If employees can be assisted to work more effectively then the organisation will out-perform the competition by delivering goods/services more effectively, of better quality and at lower cost.

Appraisal helps management to get the best out of people. Done properly, it gives greater objectivity about a person's contribution to the firm's success and, depending on the form of appraisal, there could be:

- Direct links between performance and pay
- Direct links between performance and promotion
- Direct links between performance and training

Although it is unlikely that any one appraisal scheme will attempt to address all of these issues.

OTHER ADVANTAGES

- Better employee-manager relations
- Improved employee-manager information flow about needs and expectations
- Early warning system for employee problems and grievances
- Objective schemes act as a check against discrimination and help fulfil statutory obligations on equality and fairness
- Evaluates selection and promotion procedures
- Measures effectiveness of organisational/external training schemes

HOW APPRAISAL FITS IN

ORGANISATION'S COMMERCIAL, SERVICE, QUALITY & PROFIT OBJECTIVES

ORGANISATION'S MISSION & VISION

DEPARTMENT'S MISSION & OBJECTIVES

JOB DESCRIPTION & KEY RESULT AREAS

PERFORMANCE QUALITY & PERSONAL STANDARDS

PERFORMANCE APPRAISAL

| PAY & REMUNERATION | CAREER POTENTIAL | CAREER SUCCESSION | TRAINING & DEVELOPMENT |

THE COSTS

You are not appraised because someone thinks it's a good idea or because yearly chats between you and your manager are good for morale.

Appraisal is very expensive. Say, for example, your manager has to appraise seven people and each person takes up half a day (including preparation/paperwork), that is three and a half days of management time. Multiply that by the number of managers in the organisation and you begin to see how quickly costs mount up. The H R Dept costs to co-ordinate/administer the system must be added too. This money is regarded by senior management as an investment in the organisation's employees.

WHY INVEST IN APPRAISAL?

An organisation has a mission and vision of where it is going and what it wants to achieve. These then get translated into commercial, service, quality and profit objectives for a set period, usually the financial year.

In turn, departments/units set their mission and objectives which have implications for the departmental jobs. Consequently there is a direct link between what you do and how you do it and the overall objectives of your organisation. This ensures everyone in the firm is rowing in the same direction or, as they say in the USA, 'singing off the same hymn sheet'! Diagrammatically, the process looks like this...

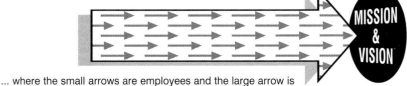

... where the small arrows are employees and the large arrow is the organisation. All work together to achieve the vision. Appraisal helps this process.

EXAMPLES OF MISSION STATEMENTS

Avis Rent A Car

> The singular vision of building the best and fastest growing company with the highest profit margins in the business of car rental through continuous investment in our network, our technology and, most of all, our people.

Xerox

> Xerox, the Document Company, will be the leader in the global document market, providing document services that enhance business productivity.

EXAMPLES OF MISSION STATEMENTS

Johnson & Johnson

" We believe our first responsibility is to the doctors, nurses and patients, to mothers and fathers and to all others who use our products and services. In meeting their needs everything we do must be of high quality. We must constantly strive to reduce our costs in order to maintain reasonable prices. Customer orders must be serviced promptly and accurately. Our suppliers and distributors must have an opportunity to make a fair profit. "

Extract from the Johnson & Johnson Credo

APPRAISALS:
WHAT & BY WHOM?

CRITERIA

To be fair and effective the appraisal has to meet:

- Agreed objective standards of work
- Agreed ways of measuring work

You **must** know about both of these and how they work in your particular system. Standards must be the same for all and be understood by all. They give:

- Objectivity and fairness in performance comparisons
- Agreed performance targets about what is/is not acceptable
- Improved fairness because appeals can be made on the basis of facts rather than on feelings or subjective judgements

Setting standards can be difficult because of the nature of the job. However, it is possible in most cases to come to an understanding about what is required. The usual question is 'What would happen or go wrong if this person did not do their job properly?' This question gives you a clue as to where to begin to find performance standards for your job.

APPRAISALS: WHAT & BY WHOM?

PERFORMANCE STANDARDS

To be effective, work standards should meet as many of the following criteria as possible:

- Make a difference to success or failure in the job
- Be mainly within the control of the person doing the job
- Be observable, measurable and objective rather than subjective
- Allow for changes in priorities and environments (especially more senior jobs)
- Enable two or more holders of the same or similar jobs to be compared with one another, fairly and equitably
- Open to third party examination should there be a difference of opinion (a third party could be a trade union steward, a staff representative, an independent senior member of management, or an Appeals Committee)

HARD & SOFT CRITERIA

Good appraisal is as objective as possible so you should be appraised essentially for what you have done or not done - ie: for those aspects of your job which can be seen, measured or directly inferred as a direct result of your behaviour at work.

There are 'HARD' criteria such as numbers of units produced, sales achieved, time keeping and quality levels.

And there are 'SOFT' criteria such as effectiveness, creativity, team contribution and client service. These criteria are more difficult to measure but there should be definitions that are available to you.

It is **very important** for you to discover what the criteria are that you are going to be appraised on.

EXAMPLES OF APPRAISAL CRITERIA

Accuracy

Achievements

Attendance

Attitude to work

Cost control

Creativity

Customer awareness

Effort

Initiative

Job knowledge

Management ability

New customers won

Number of errors, returns or complaints

Number of units produced

Potential

Punctuality

Quality of work

Relationships with staff/customers

Reliability

Sales achievement

Self-development

Service to clients

Supervisory skills

Team contribution

Time keeping

27

WHO YOU CAN BE APPRAISED BY

You can be appraised by anyone who has direct experience of your work or who is affected by it in some way.
If you like, the 'stakeholder' in your job.
The major players are:

1 Your manager

2 Yourself

3 Your fellow employees

4 Your subordinates

5 Your customers or clients

WHO YOU CAN BE APPRAISED BY

❶ YOUR MANAGER (OR MANAGEMENT)

This is the most common form of appraisal. Usually your immediate boss takes responsibility for reviewing your work but sometimes it's your boss' boss or your departmental head.

If you don't do your job properly your manager's performance will dip, so he/she has a vested interest in you doing well. Also your manager usually has most organisational day-to-day contact with you and will know what is required and how you have done. It's unfair to be appraised by someone who doesn't know your work.

Appraisal is not easy to do well and not all managers are good at it because of nervousness, bias or poor commitment. Moreover, if you've performed badly it's difficult for your manager to give you frank feedback on review, and then for you both to resume working together.

Often your boss' boss (the 'grandfather manager') is involved. This reduces the possibility of bias, gives you access to information as to how your job fits into the bigger picture, and ensures your boss does the appraisal well (otherwise his/her appraisal is affected!).

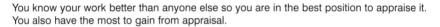

WHO YOU CAN BE APPRAISED BY
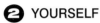 YOURSELF

You know your work better than anyone else so you are in the best position to appraise it. You also have the most to gain from appraisal.

Whatever form of appraisal you have, whatever the style of your organisation and irrespective of whether or not there is a formal role for you to play in appraisal, review your own performance so that you can have a meaningful discussion.

The more committed/motivated you are to succeed the higher the probability that you will want to get involved with your appraisal - especially when you have firm ideas about your career direction and the experience, skills and development opportunities you'd like to have.

Self-appraisal demands maturity and honesty. We tend to take personal credit for success and to blame our poor performance on external factors. It's not always easy to admit to inadequate performance.

WHO YOU CAN BE APPRAISED BY

 YOUR FELLOW EMPLOYEES

This form of appraisal is growing in popularity, mainly brought about with the increased emphasis on multifunctional teams and decentralised decision-making. If your senior management operates in what's called a matrix structure (basically an organisation with fewer managers and project orientation towards work) then peer group appraisal will probably form part of your assessment.

It does not work in situations where there is competition between employees for promotion, rewards or benefits. Moreover there is frequently a tendency to think your colleagues are good but not quite as good as you! This colleague review system also makes it difficult to maintain confidentiality. However, where it has worked successfully the morale and team performance have been exceptional.

WHO YOU CAN BE APPRAISED BY

④ YOUR SUBORDINATES

This might sound very modern but in fact it is an old principle. Students in some Italian universities in the middle ages used to select and assess their lecturers.

Subordinate appraisal provides useful information on management and leadership style and is especially beneficial when feedback is received from more than one person.

The difficulties with this approach are obvious:

- 'I'm not sure I can give my boss a bad appraisal and then have to work with him or her for the rest of the year'
- It might encourage managers to go for popularity rather than the rigours of getting a tough job done

WHO YOU CAN BE APPRAISED BY

 YOUR CUSTOMERS AND/OR CLIENTS

Customers' views are ultimately the most important so feedback here is especially beneficial. Customers are not just those outside the firm who buy products or services but also those who receive the results of your labours (eg: personnel people `work for' operational people and operational people 'work for' the sales force).

This type of appraisal is less likely to be cluttered up with personality differences and subjective views because you are being judged on outcomes rather than processes - the results rather than how you achieve them. However, it could be argued that `at-work behaviour', such as team support and commitment, is just as important as results. It is not just what you do 'it is the way that you do it'.

360° APPRAISAL

This form of appraisal is growing in popularity as firms and organisations become closer to customers and suppliers, and form strategic alliances with one another.

Information about your performance from as many sources as possible is the principle here, so it will be a combination of all those who are stakeholders in your job:

- You
- Your manager
- Your team members
- Your subordinates
- Your customers

Just as you can never have enough of a good thing so you can never have enough information about yourself and your work performance, but initially you might go into information overload!

MANAGER TRAINING IN APPRAISAL

Because appraisal is so important and has to be done well for all parties to gain the maximum benefit, your manager should receive proper training covering:

- Objectives of the appraisal scheme
- Standards of performance
- Competences and their definition
- What constitutes fair appraisal
- The paperwork system to support appraisal
- How to arrange the interview

- Rapport, questioning and listening skills
- How to give and receive feedback
- How to give difficult/good news
- How to agree/set work objectives
- How to agree/set action plans
- How to make an appeal

Better organisations will also arrange coaching, mentoring and counselling skills programmes to ensure that on-the-job training opportunities are identified and people have the right environment to give of their best.

FAIRNESS CRITERIA

To be fair, your appraisal must pass the following criteria:

1. Be undertaken by someone who knows your work
2. Review should be for the whole period not just the highlights
3. Assessed against previously agreed standards
4. Be confidential
5. Enjoy integrity and honesty
6. Not involve the disciplinary procedure
7. Provide for an appeal where there is a significant difference of opinion

FAIRNESS CRITERIA

1. BY SOMEONE WHO KNOWS YOUR WORK
You cannot have your work reviewed by someone who has no contact or knowledge of your day-to-day performance. This is essential (see page 29).

2. THE REVIEW SHOULD BE FOR THE WHOLE PERIOD
Your performance should be reviewed for the whole period, not just the last month or so. Also, the review must give the complete picture, not just 'golden moments'/'disaster dips'. You can't judge a film by the trailer nor a book by its cover.

3. ASSESSMENT AGAINST AGREED STANDARDS
It's unfair if the goal posts move during the appraisal period without your knowledge. You must know what is expected of you (performance and quality wise) so you can be responsible for your work.

4. CONFIDENTIALITY
Information on your performance should be available only to those who need it for the direct benefit of yourself/organisation. If you decide to release information, that's your concern.

FAIRNESS CRITERIA

5. INTEGRITY AND HONESTY
There should be frankness on both sides and what is said and agreed should be written up, fairly reflecting the whole discussion.

6. APPRAISAL NOT DISCIPLINE
It's unfair to go in expecting an appraisal and suddenly discover you're being disciplined. Similarly, information exchanged at appraisal shouldn't be used later in disciplinary meetings. Both processes must be completely separate.

7. APPEAL OPPORTUNITY
If you feel strongly that your appraisal wasn't fair, comprehensive or was inadequate, you must be able to appeal to someone. He/she should be senior to your appraiser, completely independent of you both, and not previously involved in the process. You must agree to the outcome whatever that may be. If two people, one who knows you/your work and another who has independently examined the evidence, reach the same conclusion then accept this as powerful feedback.

ENSURING FAIRNESS

In appraisal there are four sides to establishing fairness as far as the criteria are concerned:

1. Relevant to your job

2. Agreed and understood

FAIR CRITERIA

3. Valid

4. Observable

1. RELEVANT TO YOUR JOB Judgements about your performance must be about the essential parts of your job. It would be inappropriate, say, to use the same criteria to judge a receptionist as you would a secretary or vice versa. So to be fair the criteria should be relevant to the specific job - your job.

2. AGREED AND UNDERSTOOD Obviously your manager will have the last word about what he/she thinks should be the significant parts of your job. But a preliminary discussion about what is going to be assessed will help both sides. The last thing you want is to discover you are being assessed on something you did not know about and could have actioned if only you had known six months beforehand.

ENSURING FAIRNESS

3. VALID   Irrespective of what system is used the assessment should be as objective as possible, reflecting a true picture of the situation. Two different managers should come to the same conclusions if they supervised your work. In this way your appraisal would be valid.

4. OBSERVABLE   Your appraisal should be on those aspects of your work that can be seen or directly inferred. You can't for instance be marked down on 'team contribution' if your manager cannot give specific examples where your contribution has not been up to standard. Statements such as 'well you're just not a team player' or 'you seem not yourself in team situations' are not good enough because they are subjective and too general. Your behaviour not only has to be seen to be believed but it also has to be seen to be assessed.

It is fairer to put on the appraisal form 'no contra indications' which means not enough information to make a judgement either way.

PERFORMANCE & MEASUREMENT

PERFORMANCE & MEASUREMENT

METHODS OF PERFORMANCE MEASUREMENT

Measuring performance is not easy; so many factors are involved. It would be wonderful if there were standard rules, gauges or measures for performance but unfortunately no such instruments are available.

However, there are some excellent methods of measurement and these include:

1. Ranking
2. Narrative
3. Scales
4. Graphic rating

Note: Each method has advantages and difficulties.
There is no one perfect system. Your appraisal will depend on the style of
your organisation, working procedures and environment and on your product or service.

Remember, however imperfect the system, performance appraisal is better than no feedback at all.

PERFORMANCE & MEASUREMENT

METHODS

1. RANKING

A simple system. Each person is compared with others in the team on a criterion and given a place/rank - 1st, 2nd, 3rd, etc. Eg: 5 people (Messrs Brown, Green, Black, White, Grey) are assessed on: speed of work, quality of work, and co-operativeness. If on speed of work Mr Brown was ranked better than Mr Green who was better than Mr Black who was better than Mr White who was better than Mr Grey, the chart would look like this:

Speed of work			Speed	
1st	Mr Brown		Brown	1
2nd	Mr Green	*or like this*	Green	2
3rd	Mr Black		Black	3
4th	Mr White		White	4
5th	Mr Grey		Grey	5

If we include rankings on quality and co-operativeness, the full picture could then be:

	Speed	Quality	Co-operativeness	Total
Brown	1	3	3	7
Green	2	1	5	8
Black	3	2	1	6
White	4	5	2	11
Grey	5	4	4	13

METHODS

1. RANKING CONTD...

Mr Brown	7
Mr Green	8
Mr Black	6
Mr White	11
Mr Grey	13

The chart on page 43 shows that whilst Mr Green is excellent in quality (1) and good on speed (2) he is not that co-operative (5). Now compare each person's performance by adding each person's scores for each of the 3 criteria (Total column):

The best employee overall is the one with the lowest score. Second best has the next lowest score and so on. The final rankings are:

1st	Mr Black
2nd	Mr Brown
3rd	Mr Green
4th	Mr White
5th	Mr Grey

In appraisal the following observations might be made:

Mr Black: Good overall performance but could work a little more quickly, as Mr Brown does.

Mr Green: Good speed/output but need for discussion about lack of co-operativeness.

Mr Grey: Needs considerable help because not as good as his colleagues in all 3 areas. (NB: His performance may be acceptable in absolute standards, even though he is last compared with his colleagues. It certainly does not mean he should be disciplined for poor performance.)

METHODS

2. NARRATIVE

Here your manager writes a brief essay about your year's
performance - a `state of play' report or `internal reference'
for you. These are hard to do, take ages to write
and so are not popular.

Narrative appraisal is also difficult to assess as in its purest
form no mark is given and it is hard for an outsider to make
an accurate assessment of the individual within the total
context of the job.

> Essays can conclude with an overall
> grading/comment, as our printout here shows:

This appraisal method is the most subjective of all
since your manager selects those aspects of your
performance he/she thinks appropriate.
You may have worked hard and successfully in one
area but this could be overlooked. Added to this, not
all managers can express themselves well on paper -
hence narrative quality/value are likely to be marginal.

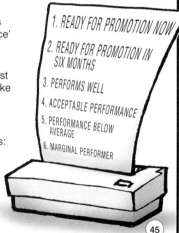

1. READY FOR PROMOTION NOW

2. READY FOR PROMOTION IN SIX MONTHS

3. PERFORMS WELL

4. ACCEPTABLE PERFORMANCE

5. PERFORMANCE BELOW AVERAGE

6. MARGINAL PERFORMER

METHODS

3. SCALES

Important parts of your job are given a scale and your performance is given a score. (Note, this is not the same as ranking your performance.)

For example, your appraisal form could look like this with 1 being good and 6 being poor:

Speed of work	1	2	(3)	4	5	6
Quality of work	(1)	2	3	4	5	6
Communication skills	1	2	(3)	4	5	6
Team attitude	1	(2)	3	4	5	6
Commitment	1	(2)	3	4	5	6
Attendance	(1)	2	3	4	5	6

METHODS

4. GRAPHIC RATING

If, for example, your job requires you to deal with people, a Behavioural Criteria Rating Scale could look like this with the criteria and rating definitions:

Criteria   Dealing with people.

Rating   Excellent   Is popular. People seek out his/her company.
definition   Easy conversationalist. Attentive and speaks well at meetings.

              Average   Comfortable with others. Finds something to say when
                        conversation lulls. Will exchange information.

              Poor   Prefers own company. Frequently lost for words.
                        Doesn't initiate conversations. Appears embarrassed when
                        speaking in front of others.

While very fair, this system entails a huge task to describe all the major components of a job in this way. Each job has its own appraisal manual and consequently is not the most popular form of assessment or appraisal.

MEASUREMENT PITFALLS

Making judgements about people is not easy; much can go wrong.

Whilst your manager has probably been trained in assessment it is important you are aware of the possible difficulties and help your manager avoid them.

It is in everybody's interest to get this right because all the interested parties have something to gain from a correct judgement - most of all you!

The main potential dangers are:

1.	The Halo effect	6.	Stereotyping
2.	The Horns effect	7.	Prejudice
3.	High/low standards	8.	Recency
4.	Centralism	9.	Golden moments
5.	Bias and preference	10.	The big bang

PERFORMANCE & MEASUREMENT

MEASUREMENT PITFALLS

1. THE HALO EFFECT

In one area you may get a high rating. However, this can `spill over' to affect other ratings which are marked higher than they should be because they bask in the golden reflection of the halo. For instance, your output may be fantastic but your teamwork not so good. Your true mark (with 10 being the highest) is:

Production   9
Team commitment   4

But because of the halo effect you may be marked as:

Production   9
Team commitment   6
(+2 because of your high production score)

2. THE HORNS EFFECT

The reverse of the halo effect. Suppose you do badly on one criteria, say attendance, but your output (production) is excellent and you are an effective/popular member of the production team. Your true mark (with 10 being the highest) is:

Production   8
Team commitment   8
Attendance   2

But your ratings given are:

Production   5
Team commitment   5
Attendance   2

Your attendance score of 2 (the Horns) has `blackened' your other scores.

(49)

MEASUREMENT PITFALLS

3. HIGH/LOW STANDARDS
Some managers have very high standards and may be 'tough' in their appraisals; others will be 'soft' and more generous. Having the 'grandfather' manager (your boss' boss) involved, will act as a moderating influence and ensure parity and fairness in assessments.

4. CENTRALISM
Most people tend to ignore either end of a scale and go for the middle. The report that says 'average' or 'satisfactory' does not mean very much. Rather than have a range with an odd number - such as 1 to 5 or 1 to 7 where there is a definite middle number (3 in 1 to 5 and 4 in 1 to 7) - better appraisal schemes have even numbers (1 to 4, 1 to 6, 1 to 8) so that a middle position is denied to the assessor.

5. BIAS
Each of us is biased. We like some people or get on with them better than others. Bias is natural but can be damaging in appraisal. If your manager likes/dislikes you this might affect your appraisal and be reflected in your assessment.

MEASUREMENT PITFALLS

6. STEREOTYPING

Stereotyping is where women are seen as not assertive enough, blacks as not giving work sufficient urgency, Irish as not being bright, English as not showing enough emotion, etc - all completely fallacious.

Stereotyping is more likely to occur when your manager is not in close contact with you/your work. The danger is your manager could fall back on what he/she imagines will be your approach rather than what it is really like.

7. PREJUDICE

This is extreme stereotyping: your manager thinks women don't make good managers, or men can't be trusted to work with small children, or that southerners are soft and northerners uncouth.

You are put in a pre-made performance box and whatever you do that shows you don't fit in that box is ignored, explained away or discredited (eg: 'you had special help or you were lucky; your input or effect was minimal/incidental because it would have happened anyway').

MEASUREMENT PITFALLS

8. RECENCY

In some appraisal schemes a year or 18 months may elapse between appraisal interviews. You/your manager will find it easier to remember what happened last week rather than what happened last month/year. A real difficulty of appraisal is that feedback can be `saved up' for the interview when it is much better given soon after the performance or work behaviour. Good or bad behaviour, the principle holds good. If you are appraised just on your last 3 months' work, in an annual appraisal scheme 75% of your efforts/commitment will be ignored.

9. GOLDEN MOMENTS

Although beneficial to you in the short term, simply recalling the best or `golden moments' of your work will miss the whole picture, and so deny you an opportunity of improvement or comprehensive feedback.

10. THE BIG BANG

This is where during the past performance period you did something spectacular (good or bad) and this is the only thing discussed at the review. Appraisal is about improving and developing your normal day-to-day performance rather than one specific thing.

PERFORMANCE & MEASUREMENT

BEHAVIOURAL CRITERIA RATING SCALES

In an attempt to ensure parity and minimise subjectivity your job can be broken down into specific behavioural statements which you either do or do not achieve. They should be typical for your job and as specific as possible. Illustrations of acceptable/unacceptable behaviour (sometimes called competencies) should be available to you. Your appraiser cannot therefore be subjective because either you have met the requirement or you have not.

This system is simple to use but there are some difficulties. First, the categories may not fit your specific job. Sometimes you get a `one size fits all' phenomena when one form of assessment sheet is used for many different job types and categories. It will also be necessary for your manager to be able to explain and illustrate why you got the markings that you did.

BEHAVIOURAL CRITERIA RATING SCALES
CENTRALISING

If I told you I'm an 80 and 190 it won't mean anything until you know the first is kilograms and the second is centimetres. Similarly, getting a 2 for 'team contribution' does not itself mean anything; your manager should be able to explain, illustrate and justify the mark.

There is also a tendency for managers `to go for the middle', sometimes known as `centralising' or `average biasing'. To overcome this, better schemes have 4, 6 or 8 points on their scale in an attempt to polarise or get a good/bad result. Even with a 6 point as a scale I have seen managers circle an imaginary 3.5 right in the middle!

TYPES OF PERFORMANCE

Each appraisal scheme will have its own definitions of what constitutes good and bad performance so what follows should be taken as an overview or guide.

Commonly there are five grading categories used to judge performance:

1. Unsatisfactory or poor
2. Marginal or just acceptable
3. Adequate, or average or acceptable
4. Good or superior
5. Excellent, outstanding or very good, obvious to all

Check on the number/definitions of gradings in your scheme.

Sometimes people get upset unnecessarily if they have not achieved a ranking of good or superior. Remember, acceptable means what it says - your work is acceptable.
Few people are marked excellent; you will see why when you look at the definitions.

TYPES OF PERFORMANCE

1. UNSATISFACTORY OR POOR

Examples and definitions of this category could include:

- Continually makes mistakes or errors
- Cannot be left unsupervised
- Often absent and/or late
- Endangers self and others
- Has poor relations with colleagues
- Unable to complete tasks
- Unable to follow instructions
- Cannot see errors in own work

Note: Disciplinary procedures and appraisal procedures are and should be quite separate. However, it would be surprising if someone described in any of the examples above did not also find themselves receiving a disciplinary interview. But, your manager would be ill advised to treat your appraisal interview as the first stage of a disciplinary interview. If this occurs pursue the matter through the appropriate appeals procedure. More importantly, improve your performance!

TYPES OF PERFORMANCE

2. MARGINAL OR JUST ACCEPTABLE

Examples and definitions of this category could include:

- Has difficulty in completing work
- Makes occasional errors of work, judgement and/or quality
- Usually takes longer to perform tasks than others in same job
- Needs regular supervision
- Sometimes misunderstands instructions
- Does not always enjoy good relations with others
- Frequently late or absent
- Sometimes unable to achieve quality standards

TYPES OF PERFORMANCE

3. ADEQUATE, AVERAGE OR ACCEPTABLE

Examples and definitions of this category could include:

- Usually completes work on time and to standard
- Takes on new work readily
- Able to understand and apply instructions properly
- Not usually late or absent from work
- Gets on well with co-workers and clients
- Can work with minimum supervision
- Makes few errors
- Displays helpful and constructive attitude

TYPES OF PERFORMANCE

4. GOOD OR SUPERIOR

Examples and definitions of this category could include:

- Continually works/produces better than others doing same job
- Works faster and achieves higher standards than most employees
- Can work unsupervised
- Only rarely late or absent
- Always pleasant and positive and popular with co-workers and clients
- Adept at more complex tasks than is normal for employees in this grade
- Self-corrects errors
- Makes suggestions for improvements

TYPES OF PERFORMANCE
5. EXCELLENT OR OUTSTANDING

Examples and definitions of this category could include:

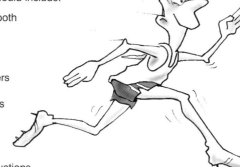

- Always exceeds standard in terms of both quality and quantity
- Exceptionally reliable and can work without supervision
- Enjoys respect/admiration of co-workers and clients; usually assumes or is nominated for informal leadership roles
- Near perfect attendance
- Continually makes recommendations for improvements
- Encourages high morale in difficult situations

FEEDBACK

ESTABLISHING AN 'OPEN' RELATIONSHIP

Two key processes will help you to achieve
an 'open' relationship:

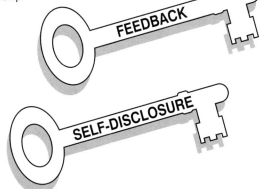

FEEDBACK

BEHAVIOUR & MOTIVATION

The more feedback you obtain about your performance the more options you will have about how you decide to behave at work in the future. Remember, what we think we do and how what we do is understood by others are two very different things. Think about a soccer referee who gives what he thinks is a fair decision - his view is not always shared by those on the terraces!

Feedback too has a very significant impact on motivation. Positive feedback usually encourages, negative feedback tends to have the opposite effect. This makes the appraising manager's job quite difficult if there are some aspects of your performance that are not up to scratch.

Your manager should be trained in how to give feedback (page 68 outlines what makes good feedback).

THE JOHARI WINDOW

Appraisal is about getting feedback on your performance at work. Obviously you know how you are doing but it is useful to get another view especially from someone who has the larger picture. Organisations change both in terms of direction and culture. If you are not made aware of these changes then you could be working very hard but in the wrong way.

There are ways of looking at ourselves at work so that we can take more control of ourselves and a more active part in our own development. The Johari Window was designed to help people think about themselves.

THE JOHARI WINDOW

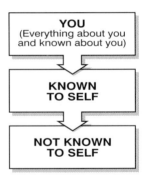

In this box there are obviously two parts ...

... all those aspects of yourself that you know about - your personal information, history, situation, etc ...

... and those aspects about you that you might not know (eg: your manager/ colleagues may know things about you/your work of which you are unaware).

THE JOHARI WINDOW

The YOU box can also be looked at in another way ...

... there is information about yourself that most people know and you are happy for them to know it ...

... and there is other information about yourself that you, for whatever reason, keep to yourself

THE JOHARI WINDOW

We can now construct the window like this:

	Known to Self	**Unknown to Self**
Known to Others	**PUBLIC** You and others know	**BLIND** Others know but you don't
Unknown to Others	**HIDDEN** You know but others don't	**UNKNOWN** You and others don't know

The boxes of the window help us to understand how we see ourselves in relation to others. In appraisal they help us understand how we see our performance in relation to our own perceptions and those of others. The windows (boundaries) can be opened as we learn more about ourselves and our performance at work.

Through appraisal, it is possible to enjoy a more 'open' relationship with our manager and vice versa. The larger the PUBLIC part of the Johari Window the stronger we become.

FEEDBACK

ESSENTIAL CONDITIONS

Specific	Feedback should be about your behaviour which can be seen and observed. It should contain specific examples of when/where you behaved in such a way.
Factual	No absolutes, eg: 'You always ...', 'Every time you ...', 'Everyone thinks ...'
Not emotional	Words like stupid, silly, hopeless, disaster should be avoided.
Directly work related	What occurs outside work and usually has no bearing on your employment/employer, has no place in appraisal feedback.
Constructive	Feedback should help/encourage/support improved performance.
Relevant to behaviour not personality	Comments such as 'you are too introverted, too aggressive and too group dependent' are inappropriate. Your manager should give specific examples. It is difficult to change one's personality but it is possible to change one's behaviour.

HOW TO RECEIVE FEEDBACK

Don't interrupt. Listen fully to the criticism and then offer a summary statement to your manager to show you have understood (but not necessarily agreed): 'So what you are saying is ...', 'You feel ...'

Think of feedback - especially when negative - as guidance and advice, an opportunity to hear how your behaviour/performance is perceived and understood by key people at work.

Ask for plenty of examples for the sake of clarity. *'Poor communication'* is an unhelpful remark; *'poor written work'* not much better. *'Your XYZ report was not easily understood because of the jargon'* is much better. Help your manager be specific.

Check out the feedback with others who know your work well and who are more likely to be frank rather than flatter you.

Where you genuinely feel the feedback is incorrect, respond calmly but assertively and give specific examples (see Appendix III on page 108).

Accept positive criticism; do not be self-deprecating.

Build into your action plan ways of working through the criticism.

Acknowledge and thank your manager for being so frank.

FEEDBACK

SELF-DISCLOSURE

This is information that you choose to reveal about yourself to help your manager understand you better. Managers can only base decisions on what they see and what they know about you.

Self-disclosure can usefully reveal information about:

Your motivations   What you enjoy and don't enjoy about work.

Your interests   What you find interesting about your work and the organisation.

Your commitments   Those that have a direct bearing on your work are especially helpful.

Your aspirations   Where you see your career going and what you want out of a job.

THE APPRAISAL STRUCTURE

THE APPRAISAL STRUCTURE

KNOW WHAT TO EXPECT

It helps to have some idea of the structure of the appraisal interview because then you know what to expect.

Lots of variations are possible, reflecting your manager's style, the scheme's purpose and, of course, your own performance. Here is a suggestion which covers all the major elements of an interview.

The purpose of the scheme is:

A   To assist the organisation do better through you improving your performance, and

B   To help you improve and thus be better prepared to achieve your career ambitions.

Your past performance is very important but the emphasis is on what needs to be improved, both for the organisation and for yourself.

THE APPRAISAL STRUCTURE

FOUR PARTS

A typical
appraisal interview
will comprise:

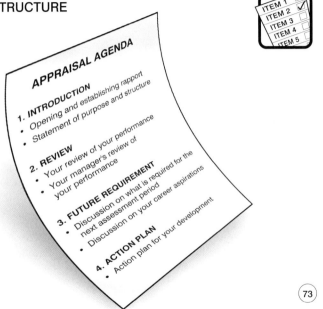

APPRAISAL AGENDA

1. INTRODUCTION
- Opening and establishing rapport
- Statement of purpose and structure

2. REVIEW
- Your review of your performance
- Your manager's review of your performance

3. FUTURE REQUIREMENT
- Discussion on what is required for the next assessment period
- Discussion on your career aspirations

4. ACTION PLAN
- Action plan for your development

THE APPRAISAL STRUCTURE

PART 1: INTRODUCTION
RAPPORT

You/your manager may feel nervous. The introduction will settle both of you down. Your manager will try to develop some rapport before turning to the business at hand. You both may talk briefly about:

- Your current project
- A social activity

- Your family
- A known interest that you have

- What you did last weekend
- Even the weather!

It is difficult for anyone to be in a high state of anxiety for a long time. This introduction will help you both relax and adjust to your surroundings and to the task at hand. It won't be that difficult because you will know a lot about the major topic for the meeting - you and your performance.

Because you will have prepared for the meeting there will be plenty to discuss and now is your opportunity.

PART 1: INTRODUCTION

APPRAISAL AGENDA

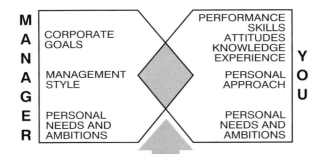

THE APPRAISAL STRUCTURE

PART 1: INTRODUCTION
STATEMENT OF PURPOSE

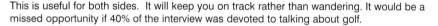

This is useful for both sides. It will keep you on track rather than wandering. It would be a missed opportunity if 40% of the interview was devoted to talking about golf.

The purpose of your appraisal could be to examine, discuss and agree:

- Pay/Bonus
- Training
- Promotion
- Development
- Change in reporting structures
- Change in job content

You will also gain information about the administration of the scheme:

I. What gets written up	IV. What actions can/can't be taken on basis of appraisal	V. How you can appeal
II. By whom		VI. Time scales
III. Who gets to see what is written		VII. And what happens next

Some or all of this might be covered in documentation you have already received but it is important for you to know the paper system as well as the process of the appraisal scheme.

THE APPRAISAL STRUCTURE

PART 2: REVIEW

SELF-REVIEW

This is your opportunity to talk about your work and your progress. As you will have prepared and perhaps practised what you might say, it will not be as difficult as you might think. When you are invited to do so here are some things you might want to say:

I.   The purpose of your job as you see it.

II. The success criteria of your job as you understand it.

III. What things have given you difficulty during the review period:
   - Why they were difficult
   - What you did to reduce the difficulty
   - What you learnt from them
   - What you will do next time to ensure they are no longer difficulties

IV. What you enjoyed and what your successes and achievements have been.

This is a lot to remember even though it concerns yourself, so it would be wise to make some notes beforehand and use them frequently.

THE APPRAISAL STRUCTURE

PART 2: REVIEW
MANAGER'S REVIEW

Since you do your job you will know more about the detail than your manager. But, your manager will know more about performance standards, quality requirements and how your job fits into the larger scheme of things. Also, because your boss has other people besides yourself to manage, your performance can be compared with that of others.

Ultimately it is your manager's view that will carry the day but it is up to you to provide as much information as you can about your job and your performance so that the appropriate decisions are made.

Expect some discussion around your view of your own performance. There will be agreements on some things and may be some differences on others.

THE APPRAISAL STRUCTURE

PART 3: FUTURE REQUIREMENT

WHAT IS REQUIRED

ITEM 1
ITEM 2 ✓
ITEM 3
ITEM 4
ITEM 5

Jobs, like organisations, continually change. Technology, competition, markets, new processes and methods ensure that nothing stays exactly the same for long.

Early 1900s　　**Mid 1900s**　　**1980s**　　**1990s**

Consequently, the way you do your job in the future might have to change. Certainly your manager will know about new targets, quality or levels of performance and these you can discuss and review together.

Many organisations have identified what competencies (skills or approaches to work) are required for different levels of work within the organisation. These can be reviewed during the interview.

THE APPRAISAL STRUCTURE

PART 3: FUTURE REQUIREMENT
CAREER ASPIRATIONS

Share with your manager the 'what next' options that you would like and hope for.

What you ask for in life and what you get are rarely one and the same. However, it is important that your manager knows about your aspirations. If you do not ask you will not get.

In these days of flatter, downsized organisations opportunities for promotion are rare and the more senior you are usually the stiffer the competition. Your manager can help you develop your experience and skills within the job so that you will be better placed for promotion or a job change.

Your manager will also give you good advice on where your career might go and how it could develop. Remember to take notes about what is said and what is agreed.

THE APPRAISAL STRUCTURE

PART 4: ACTION PLAN
PLAN FOR YOUR DEVELOPMENT

This is perhaps the most important part of the whole appraisal for you since it concerns action (no longer discussion) for the future. Together you agree on any or all of the following for the next assessment period:

- The success criteria
- The performance and quality measures required
- The personal targets for performance and quality
- Training (on the job training; external/academic programmes)
- Personal development targets (skills; experience; opportunities)

Also, organise and agree the timing of review/progress meetings to reduce risk of slippage.

Extra action by yourself may require additional resources and/or time to practise or develop your new skills. There's no point getting on a negotiation course, for instance, and then not being able to put your learning into practice.

Write down agreements made and soon after your appraisal prepare your own Action Plan (with review timings) as you see it. Pass a copy to your manager and it will help make his/her job easier.

GETTING THE BEST OUT OF APPRAISAL

GETTING THE BEST OUT OF APPRAISAL

TWO-WAY PROCESS

Appraisal is essentially a two way process between you and your manager. If you can appreciate where your manager is coming from it will make the process that much easier.

This table represents the main interests of you and your manager. The appraisal is where you meet.

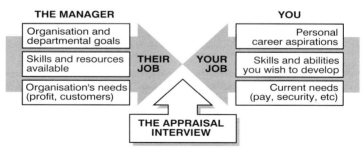

THE MANAGER		YOU
Organisation and departmental goals		Personal career aspirations
Skills and resources available	THEIR JOB / YOUR JOB	Skills and abilities you wish to develop
Organisation's needs (profit, customers)		Current needs (pay, security, etc)

THE APPRAISAL INTERVIEW

GETTING THE BEST OUT OF APPRAISAL

UNDERSTAND YOUR MANAGER

To help you understand your manager ask yourself:

- What's to be done in the department (unit, etc) for my manager to be successful?
- How will my manager know that success has been achieved?
- How will my manager be appraised?
- What are the criteria my manager uses for success?
- How well did I contribute to these important issues?
- What can I do to improve/change my job to facilitate success?

Working through these questions will help you prepare for the interview; you will be able to see it in its wider perspective.

PREPARATION

Your training, job content, pay, promotion and your career could be affected by the appraisal interview. It makes sense, therefore, to prepare thoroughly.

Only the very brilliant can walk into an exam and do well and no one can win a marathon without training. To get the best from appraisals you must be committed to thorough preparation.

This section examines:

- What information you need to prepare
- What questions you may be asked
- How to get the best from your manager

GETTING THE BEST OUT OF APPRAISAL

INFORMATION YOU NEED

Here are some of the documents that will be useful for you to have read and considered
how they apply to you and your job.

- The organisation's mission, vision and values statement
- Your job description
- Previous appraisal forms
- Your training records
- Your pay history (only if pay is to be discussed)
- Your career history with the organisation (job titles, dates, promotions, attachments, etc)
- List of your formal qualifications and courses you attended independently including
  those before you joined the organisation

GETTING THE BEST OUT OF APPRAISAL

INTERVIEW PREPARATION

- Thinking about your job
- Thinking about your performance
- Thinking about your future

Work through these categories and you will be
well prepared for the interview.

Write brief answers on a separate sheet of paper
for each of the questions that follow. You can just think
through the answers but writing them down will ensure
that your replies are better thought through. Also, come
the interview, you will find that you are far more fluent and
less likely to be lost for the right word or phrase, and you
will be able to quote examples when necessary.

INTERVIEW PREPARATION

THINKING ABOUT YOUR JOB

1. What is the main purpose of your job?

2. What would happen to your department, unit or division if you did not do your job?

3. What sort of
   A   experience
   B   qualifications
   C   skills
   are needed for someone to do your job effectively?

4. What 'competencies' or 'work/personal abilities' are needed to do your job?

5. How has your job changed in the last three years?

6. How might your job change in the future?

INTERVIEW PREPARATION
THINKING ABOUT YOUR PERFORMANCE

1. What have you done well this year (or period of assessment)?
   - Be as specific as you can, giving examples
   - Where possible quantify your successes
   - Identify the benefits to the organisation of your successes

2. What have you had difficulty achieving this year?
   - Be as specific as you can, giving examples
   - State cause of difficulty
   - Describe what you did to reduce the difficulty and what you learnt

3. This year (or period) have you:

A	Met your performance deadlines?	C	Met your project deadlines?
B	Met your quality standards?	D	Met your budget allocation?

4. What can you do this year that you couldn't do last year?
5. What have you enjoyed/not enjoyed this year?
6. What has helped and/or hindered you in your work this year?
7. Which things were easy this year and which were difficult?
8. How have you done this year compared with others doing the same job?
9. What could you do better next year?

INTERVIEW PREPARATION

THINKING ABOUT YOUR FUTURE

1. What do you see as your next job?

2. What A) experience B) skills and C) qualifications do you need to support your career aspirations?

3. Where do you see your career going - short-term, long-term?

4. Are there any immediate blockages you see in achieving your career ambitions?

5. What are you going to work on next year to improve your skills and performance and develop yourself?

6. What training would help you do your present job better?

7. What support do you need: A) from your manager B) from your colleagues C) from the organisation, to improve your current job performance?

8. What extra duties would you like to take on to improve your job interest and motivation or to develop yourself?

APPRAISAL QUESTIONS

Before looking at actual questions it will be useful to examine the type of questions you will be asked. Good questions are open, starting How?, What?, When?, Why?, Tell me... Poor questions are closed and of the either/or, rhetorical or multiple type.

Probably, your manager will talk to you differently during appraisal than at other times. Usually managers ask closed questions that get a 'yes'/'no' response (eg: Have you done that? Does it work? Have you tried so and so?). It is very effective for getting/checking information but answers are limited and not right for a career discussion.

In appraisal your manager will ask open questions which cannot be answered 'yes'/'no' but need further explanation, eg:
'**What** do you like most about the job?'
'**When** would be the best time for you to undertake the training?'
'**Tell me**, what have been your successes this year?'

APPRAISAL QUESTIONS

DEALING WITH CLOSED QUESTIONS

Some managers find it difficult to keep asking open questions and lapse into the closed kind. Should this happen, ensure that you say what is on your mind, eg:

Manager: 'Are you enjoying the job?'

You: 'Yes, I am enjoying XYZ because it gives me an opportunity to develop skills which will better prepare me for the ABC job.'

Although you have been asked a closed question you have got far more information across than just a simple 'yes' or 'no'.

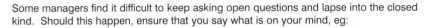

APPRAISAL QUESTIONS
EITHER/OR QUESTIONS

Some managers might unwittingly try and box you in with an either/or question when neither the 'either' nor the 'or' are appropriate.

For example, you might get asked: 'Do you want to go into market research or marketing?', when really you want to go into sales.

Since your answer will influence decisions about your future it is very important to break out of the boxes you might be put in.

So your reply could be:
'Well, those are interesting alternatives but my real interest/preference is ......'

APPRAISAL QUESTIONS

RHETORICAL QUESTIONS

Rhetorical questions almost force you to answer in a certain way by the manner in which they are asked, eg:

- 'You do need to go on a time management course, don't you?'

- 'Jim is very good at XYZ so it would be good for you to spend some time with him, wouldn't it?'

What happens if you would rather go on a self-development programme or you can't stand Jim? You could say:

- 'That is an interesting option and thank you for suggesting it but what I think might be more appropriate would be ABC because ...'

APPRAISAL QUESTIONS

MULTIPLE QUESTIONS

Where possible answer one question at a time. But, some managers in their anxiety to help will spray questions at you, eg:

● 'Would you like to talk about what you have done?   Or about your training? And what about how you fit into the new organisational structure?'

You would be at a loss to know which one to answer first.
Also if you answer one fully your manager may not
return to the other important areas of interest.
A possible response could be:

● 'You have mentioned three important
topics about my achievements, my
training and the new organisation
so perhaps we could deal with
each one at a time because each
of them is important.'

APPRAISAL QUESTIONS

Reading through the questions on page 99 onwards - even perhaps writing out answers - will help you prepare for appraisal. You will be ready with a considered response.

Your manager will comment on your performance which may be at variance with your own view. A well considered response will help you enormously in helping your manager to understand more about you at work.

Just as your manager will have thought about you, your performance and your future so you should be equally prepared.

For the sake of convenience and simplicity the questions have been put into sections but in the real interview the discussion will probably drift to and fro in a more informal way. Hopefully the questions will cover at least 80% of the subject matter of your appraisal discussion.

GETTING THE BEST OUT OF APPRAISAL

QUESTIONS YOUR MANAGER MIGHT ASK

You won't guess exactly what questions you will be asked during the interview but if you have thought through A) your job B) your performance and C) your future you will be very well prepared.

On the next pages are some questions that your manager could ask. They are divided into sections that reflect the structure and flow of the appraisal interview itself. The sections are:

1. **Rapport Questions**   To get you settled
2. **Orientation Questions**   To get both of you thinking about your job
3. **Performance Questions**   To review how you have done
4. **Development Questions**   To identify your immediate training needs
5. **Career Questions**   To discover your career aspirations

Photocopy these questions and write out your answers. By writing them down you will be able to structure your answers better and, more importantly, you will come across as confident because you are so fluent. You will present yourself as someone who takes their job and career seriously.

QUESTIONS YOUR MANAGER MIGHT ASK

1: RAPPORT QUESTIONS

- How are things going?
- What are you working on right now?
- What have you been doing lately?
- How are you getting on with the XYZ project?

QUESTIONS YOUR MANAGER MIGHT ASK

2. ORIENTATION QUESTIONS

- What have you learnt most from work this year?
- What do you think is the most significant part of your job?
- What do you think is the purpose of your job?
- How does your job fit into the overall objectives of the department (unit, division)?
- What do you think are the specific success criteria for your job?
- How does your job impact on this in the organisation?
- Who do you think your clients are?
- How do you ensure quality standards in your job?
- What do you think you would have to do to get an exceptional performance in your job?
- How do you think the way you do your job compares with others in similar positions?
- What sort of reputation do you think you enjoy in the department (unit, division)?

QUESTIONS YOUR MANAGER MIGHT ASK

3: PERFORMANCE QUESTIONS

- How do you feel you have performed this year?
- What have you found difficult this year?
- In what way has the job stretched you this year?
- How could you have performed better this year?
- In what way, if any, do you feel you have failed this year?
- What specifically has gone well for you this year?
- What objectives have you achieved this year?
  - What has helped you?
  - What has been difficult for you?
- What objectives have you not achieved this year?
  - Why do you think that was?

QUESTIONS YOUR MANAGER MIGHT ASK

4: DEVELOPMENT QUESTIONS

- What training do you think would help you to improve your job performance?
- In the year to come what will be your job objectives?
- How might you improve your job?
- What help do you need from me to do your job better?
- Which, if any, of your personal skills do you need to improve to be successful?
- What additional skills would you like to develop?
- In what way could you make a greater contribution to the job, department, organisation?
- What gives you most and least satisfaction in your job? Why?
- What help could you give to others to help them perform better?
- What do you personally want to improve on this year?

QUESTIONS YOUR MANAGER MIGHT ASK

5: CAREER QUESTIONS

- What do you see as your next job?
- Tell me about your career aspirations?
- Where would you like to be in 2, (or 5 or 10) years' time?
- What do you think your career potential is?
- What are you doing to develop your employability?
- What experience do you hope to gain to help you develop your career?
- Do you see your long-term future in this organisation?
  - If yes, doing what?
  - If no, where next?
- When do you think you might be ready for your next job or for a transfer or promotion?
- When do you think you will reach your current career goals?
- What are your career anchors?
- What really motivates you?

GETTING THE BEST FROM YOUR MANAGER

Your manager holds the key to your future. It is difficult to get promotion, a transfer, increase in resources or training without his/ her support. Do your best to get on well, therefore. Here are some tips and strategies that will help:

- Your manager has a wider perspective than you do so you too should develop a similar perspective. Work hard at seeing your job in its total context, not just how it affects you.

- See things, where possible, from your manager's viewpoint. Managers are usually able people so get behind the actions and get into their mind set.

- What people say and what people do are two different things. Watch your manager's behaviour and discover what his/her priorities are and make them yours.

- When you make a request give the context/reasons first and the benefits that the affirmative decision will bring **before** asking specifically for what you want.

APPENDICES

YOUR PRE-APPRAISAL CHECKLIST

**Photocopy this questionnaire and circle the appropriate number
(1 = complete satisfaction, 6 = great dissatisfaction/disagreement).**

Was adequate warning given of time and place of your appraisal interview?	1 2 3 4 5 6
Were you given enough time to prepare for your appraisal interview?	1 2 3 4 5 6
Were you clear before the appraisal about the success criteria, the competencies or those parts of your job about which you were going to be appraised?	1 2 3 4 5 6
Was your appraisal conducted in a friendly but business-like manner?	1 2 3 4 5 6
Were the goals and the standards of your job made clear to you during the appraisal?	1 2 3 4 5 6
Were your views and explanations welcome during the interview?	1 2 3 4 5 6
Was your performance discussed/reviewed with examples to illustrate the points made?	1 2 3 4 5 6
Was the whole review period covered by your manager, not just highlights/dips?	1 2 3 4 5 6
Did you review and agree your future performance targets?	1 2 3 4 5 6
Did you review and agree your future training requirements?	1 2 3 4 5 6
Did you discuss and review your career aspirations?	1 2 3 4 5 6
Was there sufficient time set aside for your appraisal?	1 2 3 4 5 6
Have you been encouraged to read your appraisal write up?	1 2 3 4 5 6

If you feel you have received a poor interview then in the interest of all (you, your manager, the organisation) flag your reservations using the appeal system. Remember, to appeal is very serious and you must be very specific in your feedback.

YOUR POST-APPRAISAL CHECKLIST

Photocopy this questionnaire and circle the appropriate number
(1 = complete satisfaction, 6 = great dissatisfaction/disagreement).

Was I as well prepared for the interview as I could reasonably have been?	1	2	3	4	5	6
Did I familiarise myself with the appropriate paperwork?	1	2	3	4	5	6
Did I think through my performance in readiness for the interview?	1	2	3	4	5	6
Did I think through my career aspirations in readiness for the interview?	1	2	3	4	5	6
Did I speak clearly and fluently during the interview?	1	2	3	4	5	6
Was my manner helpful and constructive towards my manager?	1	2	3	4	5	6
Was I able to give constructive suggestions to problems/opportunities identified?	1	2	3	4	5	6
Did I express my thoughts/feelings about my job and my performance?	1	2	3	4	5	6
Did I listen to and was I constructive about criticisms concerning my work?	1	2	3	4	5	6
Were my career aspirations reasonable given my skills, experience and qualifications?	1	2	3	4	5	6
Was my attitude positive and constructive during the interview?	1	2	3	4	5	6
Was I able to make realistic suggestions for my current training needs?	1	2	3	4	5	6
Was I able to make realistic suggestions for improvements to my job?	1	2	3	4	5	6
Have I developed and bought into my performance and development action plan for the next year (period)?	1	2	3	4	5	6

HOW TO DISAGREE WITH YOUR MANAGER

On occasions you and your manager will not share the same view about your performance or why something was not as it should be. It is difficult to disagree with people and certainly you do not want your appraisal to turn into an 'Oh yes you did/Oh no I didn't' argument.

What follows is no guarantee for success but you will find it works most of the time:

Say 'yes' ⟹ Show you understand ⟹ Ask permission ⟹ Give your reasons ⟹ Give your position, or ⟹ Go for a compromise.

Manager: 'Your results on the XYZ project were well below standard.'

You: 'Yes, you're right the results were worse than they could have been. I know it was important to you and the department for that project to go well. But, if I may, I would like to fill in some of the background. First the design wasn't complete and we had to start without it, and then there was the delay on the equipment being available due to a supplier problem. Finally the completion time was unexpectedly brought forward by the client. I hope you will agree that the problems were outside of my control'.

Isn't this better than just saying: 'But it was not my fault'?

THE APPRAISAL CHARTER

(FOR YOU AND YOUR MANAGER)

- Both of you should be trained in how to get the best out of the appraisal system

- Both parties need adequate time to prepare for the appraisal

- There should be a clear understanding about ...
  - Your job
  - The standards required
  - The performance measures
  ... for both you and your manager

- The employees' views and opinions are important and are an essential part of the appraisal

- Judgements must be based on demonstrable behaviour and facts arising from the work environment

- Wherever possible action plans for improvement should be mutually agreed

- Where there is a strong difference of opinion there should be an opportunity for both sides to appeal to someone who can give an independent and binding decision

About the Author

Max A. Eggert BSc,MA,CFIPD,CFAHRI,ABPS,MAPS.
Max is an international management psychologist who specialises in assisting
organisations and individuals to achieve their best. He works mainly in the UK and
Australia. A respected authority on the human and organisational aspects of change
and empowerment, Max has delivered workshops and seminars to thousands of
executives and managers throughout the world.

Max has also written: The Assertiveness Pocketbook; The Controlling Absenteeism
Pocketbook; The Motivation Pocketbook; The Perfect CV (in top 10 business books);
The Perfect Interview; The Perfect Career; The Perfect Consultant.

Contact
Max can be contacted in Australia at: Pilgrim House, 9 Quota Avenue, Chipping Norton, NSW 2170.
Tel: (61) 2 9821 1105   Fax: (61) 2 9821 1106   Mobile: 040 360 2286   E-mail: max@transcareer.com.au

About Pocketbooks

Pocketbooks are widely available from bookshops throughout the UK,
from a network of agents overseas or direct from the publisher.

The Managing Your Appraisal Pocketbook was first published in 1996 by:
Management Pocketbooks Ltd.,
Laurel House, Station Approach, Alresford, Hants SO24 9JH, U.K.
Tel: +44 (0)1962 735573   Fax: +44 (0)1962 733637
E-mail: sales@pocketbook.co.uk   Web: www.pocketbook.co.uk

Reprinted:
1998, 2000, 2001, 2003.

© Max A. Eggert 1996.

Printed in U.K.

ISBN 1 870471 38 5